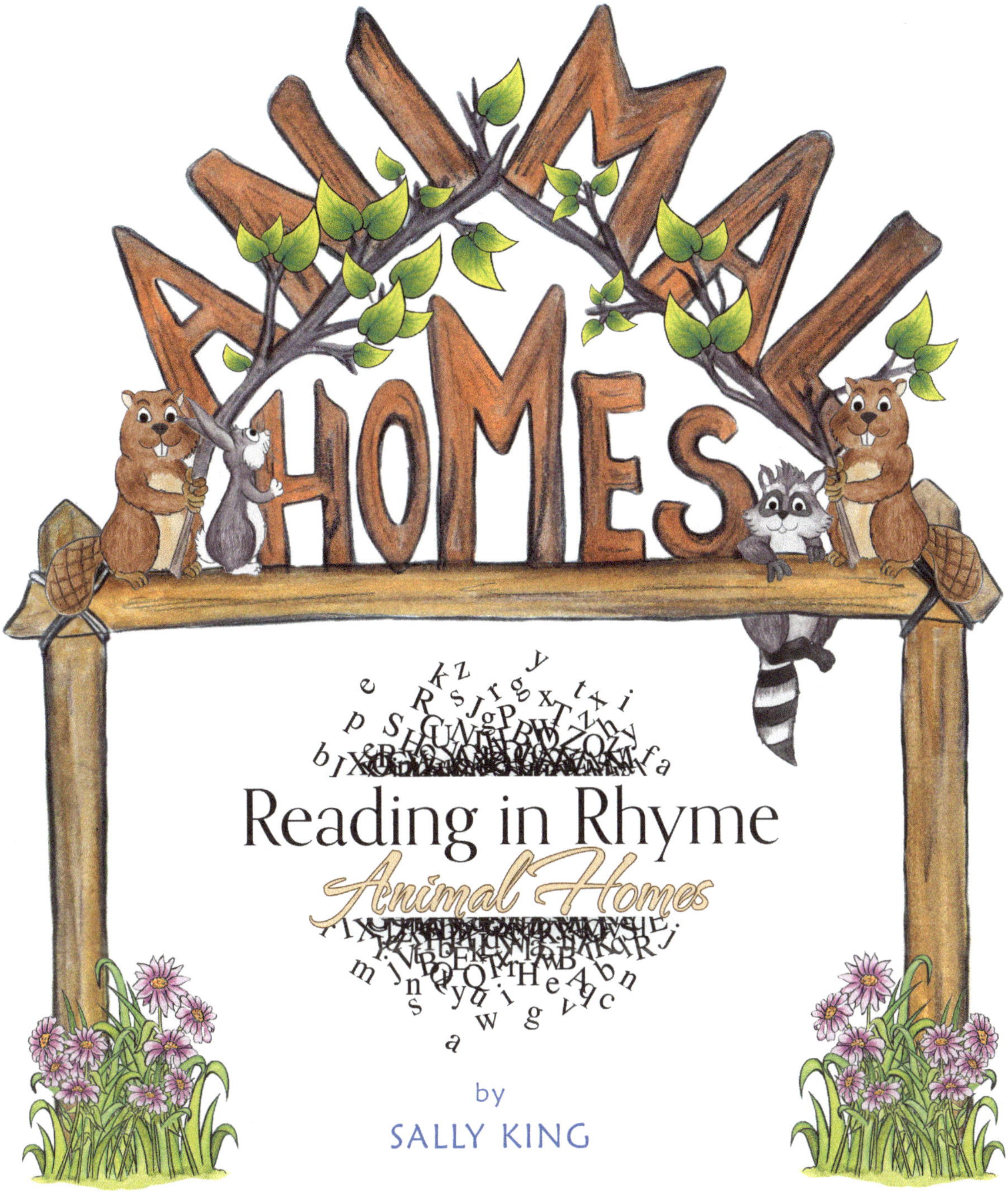

ANIMAL HOMES

Reading in Rhyme
Animal Homes

by
SALLY KING

Illustrated by: Corrina Holyoake

As big as an elephant, as small as a mouse,
Every animal needs a house!

Grosvenor House
Publishing Limited

All rights reserved
Copyright © Sally King, 2021

The right of Sally King to be identified as the author of this
work has been asserted in accordance with Section 78
of the Copyright, Designs and Patents Act 1988

The book cover picture is copyright to Sally King

This book is published by
Grosvenor House Publishing Ltd
Link House
140 The Broadway, Tolworth, Surrey, KT6 7HT.
www.grosvenorhousepublishing.co.uk

This book is sold subject to the conditions that it shall not, by way of
trade or otherwise, be lent, resold, hired out or otherwise circulated
without the author's or publisher's prior consent in any form of binding or
cover other than that in which it is published and
without a similar condition including this condition being imposed
on the subsequent purchaser.

A CIP record for this book
is available from the British Library

ISBN 978-1-83975-782-2

CONTENTS

WHO LIVES IN A NEST 1
WHO LIVES IN A DEN 2
WHO LIVES IN A BURROW 3
WHO LIVES IN A ROOST 4
WHO LIVES IN A LODGE 5-6
WHO LIVES IN A SETT 7-8
WHO LIVES IN A DREY 9
WHO LIVES IN A FORMICARY 10
WHO LIVES IN A FORM 11-12
WHO LIVES IN AN EARTH 13-14
WHO LIVES IN APIARY 15
WHO LIVES IN AN EYRIE 16
WHO LIVES IN A VESPIARY 17
WHO LIVES IN A FORTRESS 18
WHO LIVES IN A HOLT 19-20
WHO LIVES IN MEWS 21-22
WHO LIVES IN A RANARIUM 23
AS BIG AS AN ELEPHANT, AS SMALL AS A MOUSE EVERY
ANIMAL NEEDS A HOUSE 24-26

WHO LIVES IN A NEST

So many creatures choose a NEST,
A bird is the one that you know best,

But there are also ants, who gather together,
And make an ants' NEST to escape bad weather.

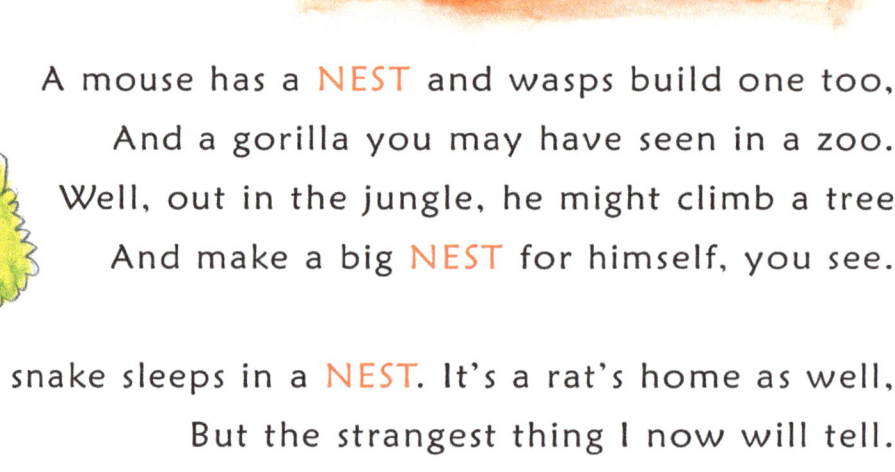

A mouse has a NEST and wasps build one too,
And a gorilla you may have seen in a zoo.
Well, out in the jungle, he might climb a tree
And make a big NEST for himself, you see.

A snake sleeps in a NEST. It's a rat's home as well,
But the strangest thing I now will tell.
Did you know that an alligator or crocodile
Has a home called a NEST, made from a pile
Of sticks and rushes found in the lake
Or the river? Well, for goodness sake!

So a NEST is a home for a rat or a mouse,
Not you! You most probably live in a house!

WHO LIVES IN A DEN

Have you ever built a DEN in the woods for fun?
Using sticks and leaves?
Sleep there when done?

Well, a bear and a lion both do the same.
They build themselves a DEN.
It might be in a cave hidden away
To be safe from hunters, or when
Their families move in to stay,
Or their cubs are born
And need somewhere to play.

A DEN is the house of a lion or bear,
A secret place, a home to share.

So when you next build with your friends
A secret place that's new,
Remember the animals making their dens,
In exactly the same way as you.

A bear, or a lion, woodland animals do,
A racoon is another, to name just a few.

WHO LIVES IN A BURROW

Many animals dig a hole. They can be found
Burrowing down far under the ground,
To hide from enemies who would do them harm,
Or simply, in winter, to keep themselves warm.

Rabbits live in BURROWS as families together,
Keeping safe and snug in all kinds of weather,

But a BURROW is home to another you know,
An animal called an armadillo.

Such an animal you may never have met
Or had in your house as a family pet.

He has a leathery armour shell
Of bony plates wrapped around him well.

He sleeps in a BURROW for most of the day
And very rarely comes out to play.

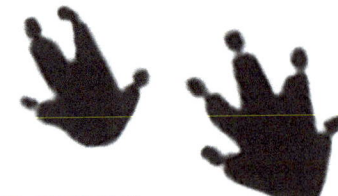

So when someone asks you, "Who lives in a BURROW?"
You can now answer, "An armadillo!"

WHO LIVES IN A ROOST

Bats live in a ROOST, hanging upside down
From trees or rafters up high,
Nocturnal, they wake and hunt at night,
Swooping across the sky.

A colony of bats roosting together
Can be an eerie sight,
All sleeping with folded wings,
Yet coming alive at night.

We think of chickens roosting in coops,
Settling down to sleep on a perch,

Bats do the same, sleep during the day,
In the high bell tower of a church.

That's why we call the home a ROOST,
Somewhere dusty, dark and high,
Where he hangs to snooze in peace and quiet,
Then at night comes out to fly.

WHO LIVES IN A LODGE

A LODGE can be a house made of wooden planks
Cut from trees or logs alongside river banks,

This is exactly what Beaver makes,
A "master builder" in our streams and lakes!

He gnaws through a tree, or dams a stream,
Which creates a pond, if you know what I mean.

Right in the middle an island is made
Of branches or twigs which he carried and laid
To make a LODGE, a perfect home,
An island house where he's safe and warm.

No predator can reach him, how clever was he,
To have this idea and all made from a tree?

A beaver lives in a LODGE built by himself alone.
This is his palace!
His house!
His home!

WHO LIVES IN A SETT

A SETT is a network of tunnels and doorways
Built far under the ground,
If you see a large hole near a wood and a field,
A cete* of badgers you may have found.

Badgers like woods, to be hidden, feel safe,
But they also need grass close by,
For at night they come out and dig for worms,
A dinner their cubs might try.

A SETT can be lots of chambers and holes
For four or five families to share,
The SETT can be seen, but not often the beast,
For to see a badger itself is rare.

People live in a house or maybe a flat.
Not a burrow, a nest or a den,
Badgers live in a SETT to be safe and warm,
Away from predators, hunters and men.

a cete is the collective noun for a group or collection of badgers

WHO LIVES IN A DREY

When walking through a wood of trees,
A rustle of leaves you hear,
The scamper of feet, the glimpse of a tail,
And you know that a squirrel is near.

You hear a chatter from the branches above,
Or an acorn drops down on your head,
You catch sight of that squirrel darting away
As he races towards his bed.

He feels safe in his DREY up there so high,
A hole in the trunk of a tree,
Filled with dry leaves, soft moss and twigs,
And a collection of nuts for his tea.

A DREY is where a squirrel hides
To be safe and sheltered from storm,
This is his home, his little place,
Where he feels content and warm.

WHO LIVES IN A FORMICARY

Some creatures live in nests as you know,
Birds of all kinds, woodpecker or crow,

You've learned about rats and crocodiles, too,
Having nests as their homes, but here's something new.

We said that ants live in a nest or a hill,
But did you know there's another word still?

Ants' nest or ant hill is the usual name,
But a FORMICARY means exactly the same.

To be extremely clever or even contrary,
You can say that ants make a FORMICARY,

When in a colony they choose to stay
A FORMICARY is what you would say.

So when you are asked where ants live, please tell,
A FORMICARY - where ants in thousands dwell.

WHO LIVES IN A FORM

A FORM is a shallow dip in the ground,
Just made to shelter a hare.
If you disturb her she will race away,
Follow her if you dare!

Her powerful hind legs propel her forward,
She bounds across the grass.
Into the woods to hide away
Until she sees you pass.

Watch her go, in a zigzag pattern!
Through the field to the woodland edge,
She leaves her FORM, that dip in the ground,
Sheltered beside the hedge.

FORM can be used for a class in your school,
Or a bench you might sit upon,
But it's also a place of rest for a hare,
As she sleeps in the heat of the sun.

WHO LIVES IN AN EARTH

An EARTH is a lair a fox has made
At the base of a tree, or in scrub,
It's usually the vixen who finds the home,
When she's ready to house her cub.

A male might curl up above the ground,
His bushy tail covering his face,
A fox in a town might crawl under a shed
Or another suitable place.

Foxes like woods with lots of trees,
They are nocturnal and hunt at night,
So a sleeping place for mother and cubs
During the day would be about right.

She may dig her own, or take an old burrow
A rabbit has left behind,
Maybe an old badger sett,
Just anywhere she can find.

We live on the earth, in the solar system,
Spinning around and around,
Night and day, dark and light,
Planet earth, where life is found.

A fox has a home with the very same name,
An EARTH, dug under the ground,
In woods, under trees, amongst the ferns,
Foxes stay safe and sound.

WHO LIVES IN AN APIARY

We talk about the birds and bees,
But where do they both reside?
Birds build nests or roost in trees,
Or in a cage or aviary they hide.

Bees live in hives, large numbers together,
Bringing pollen from flowers to their queen,
The honey they make can be analysed
To see exactly where they have been.

A bee keeper may have many hives
Which he keeps in an orchard of trees,
An APIARY is the name we give
To a collection of hives for bees.

Birds in an aviary, bees in an APIARY,
We could easily make a mistake,
I've explained it to you
Without any ado,
Bee hives an APIARY make.

WHO LIVES IN AN EYRIE

An EYRIE is a lofty nest
High up in a tree, on a cliff is best.

A home made by a bird of prey,
Built out of reach and out of the way.

The eagle with his giant wing span,
Known as the King of Birds to man,

Can dip and soar throughout the day,
Then swoop and dive to meet his prey.

Returning with food to an EYRIE of chicks,
To their home that is made of moss and sticks,

An EYRIE, made by a nudge and a tweak,
So cleverly crafted by that huge, curved beak.

WHO LIVES IN A VESPIARY

Bees live in an apiary,
Wasps live in a VESPIARY,

Vespa is a Latin word,
A language you may not have heard,
The Romans spoke Latin when they came
To England, so they brought that name,

Vespa means wasp and wasps need a space
To call their home, so they build a place
Where they gather and survive,
Just like bees inside the hive,

Bees in an apiary,
Wasps in a VESPIARY,
A new word to use,
If you ever should choose.

WHO LIVES IN A FORTRESS

The word FORTRESS conjures up soldiers,
Prisons and dungeons, castles tall,
But when it is used as an animal's house,
It doesn't mean that at all.

A FORTRESS, as an animal's home,
Belongs to a busy mole,
A little chap with silver black fur,
Who loves to dig a hole!

Moles are very rarely seen,
Spending their lives underground.
In the dark, they can hardly see,
As they dig their way around.

With excellent senses of smell and touch
And little spade like claws,
A mole can dig up mountains of mud
With his velvety little paws.

His house consists of underground tunnels
And quite large hills of soil,
These hills are known as FORTRESSES,
A reward for all his toil!

WHO LIVES IN A HOLT

The word otter sounds like water,
For this is where otters are found,
And a HOLT is the home he builds himself
Near water, but underground.

His HOLT can be under a willow tree,
Beneath the branches, or in the roots,
Between two rocks, in a hole in the bank,
Wherever the waterside suits.

Otters are carnivores,
Feeding mainly on fish,
Strong swimmers and divers
They move with a swish
Of a muscular tail, sometimes a foot long,
Steering through water, so deftly, so strong.
Sunbathing on land by day,
Close to their HOLT they play,
But active at night,
They can be seen using tools,
Like beavers building in midnight pools.

WHO LIVES IN A MEWS

When we speak of MEWS we usually mean
Small bijou properties that you may have seen
In a cobbled alley tucked away
From the hustle and bustle of a city day.
Maybe nowadays they have developed as such,
But from past times they have changed very much.

Of old, these rows of buildings and stables
Were used to house birds with different labels,

Birds of prey, brought home from their flight,
Were kept in MEWS through the day and the night,

For when these birds their feathers they lose,
It was important to house them away in MEWS.

Muer is French for the verb to moult. In this case
They then were enclosed in a small, confined space.
Spare feathers would drop to the ground below
And that is called "moulting" don't you know.

Thus MEWS became the common term
For the buildings used as a falconry home.

French was a language with much influence
In England when kings rode out in hunts
To sport with trained hawks and dogs,
Hunting deer, wild pigs and hogs,

Riding through forest, royal parks and woods,
Their birds' heads covered with little hoods
Until they were ready to set free and fly
Returning to falconer by and by,

He would take his birds to their MEWS to confine,
While the hunters made merry with feast and wine.

WHO LIVES IN A RANARIUM

Puddles and ponds, pools and lakes,
If you want to raise some frogs,
Marshland, compost heaps, streams and becks,
Even swamps and bogs.
Anywhere where there is water
Becomes a home for a frog or a toad,
RANARIUM is the term we use
For an amphibian's abode.

Rana is Latin for frog,
So RANARIUM becomes the word
For the place where frogs breed and grow,
Where their repetitive croaking is heard.
You may be walking one day past a pond
With bulrushes and reeds growing tall,
If you are quiet, stand still and listen,
You might hear the bull frog's call.

    His voice travels through air and through water,
    It is here he will remain,
    This will be the place for him,
    His territory to claim.

AS BIG AS AN ELEPHANT, AS SMALL AS A MOUSE EVERY ANIMAL NEEDS A HOUSE.

You live in a home with a family to love,
But what if you were an eagle or dove?
Where would you live? In a house or a flat?
Or would you prefer a hole in the ground, or something like that?

Different animals live in different places,
And each home has a name,
You may know some, others sound strange,
Let's play a little game.

Which animal lives somewhere that sounds a bit ghostly?
Which home rhymes with best?
The eerie home belongs to the eagle.
And the rhyming word is nest.

What about a squirrel small?
Where does he live, red or grey?
Would he build a den, an earth or sett?
No! he builds a drey!

Bees together live in a hive,
You knew that already,
An apiary is made with lots of hives,
But what is a formicary?

Lots of ants build their home together
And a formicary is the result,
And birds of prey are confined in a house
When their feathers begin to moult.

Do you remember the name we give
To the falcon's resting place?
Buildings called mews are where they are housed
After their hunting race.

What about wasps? Where do they live
When they gather together in a swarm?
A vespiary is the name of their home,
The place they are safe and warm.

Then there is a fortress for the digging mole,
The form for the bounding hare,
The holt for the otter, the beaver's lodge,
Or the den for the lion or bear.

Every animal, bird, insect or fish,
Wherever they may roam,
Deserves somewhere to rest and sleep and feed,
Somewhere to call his home.

Lightning Source UK Ltd.
Milton Keynes UK
UKHW051127191021
392416UK00002B/92